THE LITTLE BOOK OF
FATHERS
& SONS

Published in 2024 by OH!
An Imprint of Welbeck Non-Fiction Limited,
part of Welbeck Publishing Group.
Offices in: London – 20 Mortimer Street, London W1T 3JW
and Sydney – Level 17, 207 Kent St, Sydney NSW 2000 Australia
www.welbeckpublishing.com

ISBN 978-1-80069-581-8

Compiled and written by: Malcolm Croft
Editorial: Victoria Denne and Saneaah Muhammad
Designer: Tony Seddon
Project manager: Russell Porter
Production: Arlene Lestrade

A CIP catalogue record for this book is available from the British Library

Printed in Dubai

10 9 8 7 6 5 4 3 2 1

THE LITTLE BOOK OF
FATHERS & SONS

A CELEBRATION
OF GROWING UP TOGETHER

CONTENTS

INTRODUCTION – 6

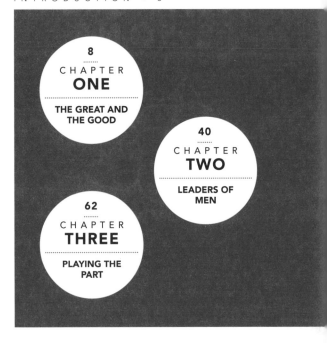

8

CHAPTER
ONE

THE GREAT AND
THE GOOD

40

CHAPTER
TWO

LEADERS OF
MEN

62

CHAPTER
THREE

PLAYING THE
PART

104

CHAPTER
FOUR

WALK THIS WAY

124

CHAPTER
FIVE

SAME GOALS

152

CHAPTER
SIX

SAME SCRIPT

INTRODUCTION

Becoming a father is the most important moment in any man's life. It is the moment when everything changes forever, and while fathers adore their daughters, the father-and-son relationship has many different dynamics, expectations, and pressures. There is no guidebook for fathers to raise their sons by - just instinct, love and, of course, passing on the traits of their own father.

A father must prepare his son for life and help him deal with the many obstacles and challenges he will face. Every father is different; some adopt a tough-love stance, while others are more laid-back. In years gone by, many fathers would put more pressures on their sons to follow in their footsteps, to be strong emotionally and physically.

The modern father is likely to be more hands-on than the fathers of yesteryear, wanting to take an active role in their upbringing and enjoying more quality time than would have been the case in the past.

The father-and-son relationship is so unique in many ways and can be incredibly special, filled with love and pride.

Sharing hobbies can be a way of creating memories that will last forever, whether playing football in the park or fishing on the banks of the river – these memories are what the son will remember long after their father has gone.

In a perfect world, every son's superhero should be their dad – somebody they aspire to be and their greatest role model.

A father's love for their son is unconditional, and the pride they have for their boy knows no bounds.

In the pages that follow there are quotes, facts and observations from all walks of life and from all over the globe that speak to the unique bond between father and son.

Whether through an ancient proverb or words from today's movie and sports stars, *The Little Book of Fathers & Sons* attempts to share the true essence of this magical relationship.

CHAPTER ONE

THE GREAT AND THE GOOD

Words of wisdom from the
wisest of wordsmiths…

66

Father! – to God
himself we cannot
give a holier name.

99

William Wordsworth

66

My little boy yesterday, my friend today, my son forever.

99

Unknown

Five traits of being a good father

1. Being open-minded

2. Accepting your son for who he is

3. Spending quality time with your son

4. Leading by example

5. Being supportive and loyal

66

When your son grows up, become his brother.

99

Arabic proverb

"

The best gift a father
can give to his son is
the gift of himself –
his time. For material
things mean little, if
there is not someone
to share them with.

"

Unknown

66

Easier to rule a nation than a son.

99

Chinese proverb

"

The son shoots a leopard; the father is proud.

"

African proverb

66

Being a great father is
like shaving. No matter
how good you shaved
today, you have to do it
again tomorrow.

99

Reed Markham
A poignant analogy from the US author

"

To be a successful father... there's one absolute rule: when you have a kid, don't look at it for the first two years.

"

Ernest Hemingway
The legendary author and father of two sons'
tongue-in-cheek advice for raising offspring

66

Whoever does not have a good father should procure one.

99

Friedrich Nietzsche

66

When I was a boy of 14, my father was so ignorant I could hardly stand to have the old man around. But when I got to be 21, I was astonished at how much the old man had learned in seven years.

99

Mark Twain

Becoming a father isn't difficult, but it's very difficult to be a father.

Wilhelm Busch

66

My father must have
had some elementary
education for he could
read and write and keep
accounts inaccurately.

99

George Bernard Shaw

66

As long as I am running, my father will still have a son.

99

Brazilian proverb

Father's Day originated in the United States of America, with the first unofficial Father's Day celebration held in Spokane, Washington, on 19 June, 1910.

> **"**
> I cannot think of any
> need in childhood as
> strong as the need for a
> father's protection.
> **"**

Sigmund Freud

66

Everyone calls his son his son, whether he has talents or has not talents.

99

Confucius

"

One of the greatest gifts you can give your teenage boy is the gift of letting him know you get it. You've been there.

"

Sebastian R. Jones
The parenting author suggests fathers reconnecting with their teenage selves can establish a common ground with their sons

66

A father doesn't tell you he loves you. He shows you.

99

Unknown

"

When you follow in the path of your father, you learn to walk like him.

"

Ghanaian proverb

"

Though our new son is barely
a part of our present, we look
at his squirming, warm bundle
of future potential and say to
ourselves, 'Hello, little man.'
Little do we know the adventure
we are beginning!

"

Dr Gregory L. Jantz
The author and psychologist on the first days of
fatherhood, Today.com, April 2023

66

It is not flesh and blood, but the heart which makes us fathers and sons.

99

Johann Christoph Friedrich Schiller
A memorable quote by the German poet,
philosopher, physician, historian, and playwright–
author of "Ode to Joy"

66

Life doesn't come with an instruction book – that's why we have fathers.

99

H. Jackson Browne
Bestselling US author – who actually did write a book called *Life's Little Instruction Book* – seems to have found a niche in the market, Today.com, April 2023

66

Good fathers make good sons.

99

Unknown

"

You don't raise heroes, you raise sons. And if you treat them like sons, they'll turn out to be heroes, even if it's just in your own eyes.

"

Walter M. Schirra Sr.
Aviator, pilot, and NASA astronaut with a touching sentiment that will ring true for many devoted fathers, Today.com, April 2023

"

One of the greatest
lessons I learned from
my dad was to make
sure your children know
that you love them.

"

Al Roker
The US presenter and journalist's simple life lessons

66

I am a family man, and my most important role is a father to my son.

99

Ed Skrein
The actor, director and screenwriter has his priorities
firmly in place, *Good Housekeeping*, April 2023

66

I once wrote, 'No love is greater than that of a father for his son.' Throughout my life, I've learned that on a daily basis from one of the best dads ever. Happy Father's Day to my Dad and all of the other great fathers out there.

99

Dan Brown
The author pays tribute to his dad with this touching
Facebook post, Facebook, June 2017

66

One father is more than a hundred schoolmasters.

99

English proverb

66

Never fret for an only son, the idea of failure will never occur to him.

99

George Bernard Shaw

CHAPTER TWO

LEADERS
OF MEN

How some of the most
respected men in the world
view the father-and-son
relationship…

66
Pa, we're all so proud of you.
99

HRH Prince William
The heir to the British throne addressed the gathered
crowd and his father, King Charles, at the Coronation
concert, BBC News Twitter feed, May 2023

66

I have found the best way to give advice to your children is to find out what they want and then advise them to do it.

99

Harry S. Truman
The former US President's open-minded approach to fatherhood

Ramjit Raghav from
India became the world's
oldest dad in 2012 when
he fathered his second
child... aged 96!

"

My father's values and vision
of this country obviously form
everything I have as values and
ideals. But this is not the ghost
of my father running for the
leadership of the Liberal party.
This is me.

"

Justin Trudeau
Canadian Prime Minister, carving his own path,
but following in his father Pierre's footsteps

"

There's no advice like fathers' – even if you don't take it.

"

American proverb

"

Perhaps it's the newfound clarity
I have as a father, knowing that
my son will always be watching
what I do, mimicking my
behaviour, one day maybe even
following in my footsteps.

"

HRH Prince Harry

66

One night a father overheard his son pray: Dear God, make me the kind of man my daddy is. Later that night, the Father prayed: Dear God, make me the kind of man my son wants me to be.

99

Unknown

66

Every father should remember one day his son will follow his example, not his advice.

99

Charles F. Kettering
The inventor's poignant observation on the father-and-son relationship, Today.com, April 2023

66

My strong determination for justice comes from the very strong, dynamic personality of my father... I have rarely ever met a person more fearless and courageous than my father.

99

Martin Luther King Jr.
The civil rights leader and activist pays tribute to his father, Atlanta pastor Martin Luther King Sr, *The Autobiography of Martin Luther King Jr.*, 1998

66

I believe that what we become depends on what our fathers teach us at odd moments, when they aren't trying to teach us. We are formed by little scraps of wisdom.

99

Umberto Eco
The Italian philosopher takes a different view on the father-and-son learning mechanism

"

The greatest gift I ever had came from God; I call him Dad!

"

John W. Bratton
US composer

❝

When a father gives to his son, both laugh. When a son gives to his father, both cry.

❞

Yiddish proverb

"

Thinking that it hadn't affected me at all, then later in my life realising it was probably the defining moment of my life really. It's kind of defined my personality. It's as simple as something so precious being taken from you, you can feel very insecure. Just to make sure people aren't going to abandon you.

"

Bob Mortimer

The UK comedian recalls how losing his father unexpectedly as a youngster shaped him into the person he became, *Irish News*, February 2019

"

Tiger father begets tiger son.

"

Chinese proverb

66

Like father like son: Every good tree maketh good fruits.

99

William Langland

66

Until you have a son of your own, you will never know what that means. You will never know the joy beyond joy, the love beyond feeling that resonates in the heart of a father as he looks upon his son.

99

Kent Nerburn
The US author is evidently a very happy father!

66

If the relationship of father
to son could really be reduced
to biology, the whole earth
would blaze with the glory of
fathers and sons.

99

James Baldwin
US author of such classics as
Go Tell It on the Mountain

66

When you teach your son, you teach your son's son.

99

The Talmud

"

A father carries pictures where his money used to be...

"

Unknown

Twelve classic songs about fathers and sons

1. "Father and Son" – Cat Stevens
2. "Song for Dad" – Keith Urban
3. "Letter to Me" – Brad Paisley
4. "He Didn't Have to Be" – Brad Paisley
5. "My Father's House" – Bruce Springsteen
6. "Dance with My Father" – Luther Vandross
7. "Hell Yeah" – Neil Diamond
8. "Dear Father" – Neil Diamond
9. "Who You'd Be Today" – Kenny Chesney
10. "Father and Son" – Phil Collins
11. "Cat's in the Cradle" – Harry Chapin
12. "The Living Years" – Mike & The Mechanics

CHAPTER THREE

PLAYING THE PART

Fatherhood and being a son –
Hollywood style…

66

My father never believed in me! I'm not gonna make the same mistake. From now on I'm gonna be kinder to my son and meaner to my dad.

99

Homer Simpson

66

Ray may have a problem with being a little too good-looking. Looks exactly like Rebecca. When he was born, he looked like one of the farmers in *The Magnificent Seven*. He does move like me. There's a lot of body language on him. You don't miss them Nicholson legs. Somebody's got to get them, poor thing. They're useful but short. Most infants pretty much don't have chins. But Ray always had a jaw.

99

Jack Nicholson
The Hollywood legend on his son Ray – and the fact that short legs run in the family! PopSugar.com, June 2021

It is estimated that
one in every 250 births
results in a father
becoming the dad of
twins – and the chance of
having twin boys is 50%

"

I got really lucky in that my dad stopped working just as I started. He took a few years off, not on purpose, but he has three sons with his wife of 30 years, and he wanted to be involved with them. As much as I missed him being around when I was growing up, I think he missed us too and he wasn't going to let that happen again.

"

Kiefer Sutherland
The actor reflects on his relationship with his father,
Hollywood star Donald Sutherland, IMDB.com

"

Mean fathers,
wasteful sons.

"

French proverb

> **"**
>
> # The father who does not teach his son his duties is equally guilty with the son who neglects them.
>
> **"**

Confucius

"

Jaden is 100% fearless, he will do anything. So as a parent it's scary, it's really terrifying – but he is completely willing to live and die by his own artistic decisions and he just doesn't concern himself with what people think.

"

Will Smith
The Hollywood star on son Jaden, also making his way in acting, HuffPost.com, September 2021

"

I definitely would do another one, absolutely. You know how Johnny Depp and Tim Burton always do movies together, Martin Scorsese and Leonardo DiCaprio? We'll have a relationship like that.

"

Jaden Smith
Jaden discusses working with his father Will in the movie *After Earth*, MTV.com, May 2013

66

We worked together on
Tucker: The Man and His Dream
by Francis Ford Coppola a few
years before this, but we had
a lot more scenes to play in
Blown Away, and I remembered
something that I had forgotten,
how much fun it was to work
with my dad, because you
become peers all of a sudden,
especially if you approach the

work in the same way, and you get back to that childlike thing of playing with each other, you become these two big kids and you get excited about ideas that you want to try. You are literally playing, and it's great to do that with your father.

Jeff Bridges
Jeff Bridges reflects on the fun of working with his dad,
Lloyd Bridges, GoldenGlobes.com, November 2020

66

He was a pretty good kid. Not
much of a problem. His mother
gave him a lot of values, because
she's a good person.

99

Clint Eastwood
on son Scott Eastwood, Esquire.com, August 2016

66

My father's definitely old-school.
And he raised me with integrity
– to be places on time, show up,
and work hard.

99

Scott Eastwood
on his father – Hollywood legend Clint Eastwood,
Esquire.com, August 2016

66

Dad, your guiding hand on my shoulder will remain with me forever.

99

Unknown

Top ten father and son films

1. The Road
2. Field of Dreams
3. Bicycle Thieves
4. Road to Perdition
5. Catch Me If You Can
6. Honey Boy
7. Big Fish
8. Indiana Jones and the Last Crusade
9. The Pursuit of Happyness
10. The Godfather

Movieweb.com

66

Every son's first superhero is his father, and it was the same for me. For me, he was Superman and Batman combined.

99

Tiger Shroff
The Indian acting star marvels at his
very own superhero…

66

Unlike a lot of actors, my father encouraged his kids to go into showbiz. He loved all the aspects of show business: knowing the crews, the travelling, the adventures you get involved in. He revelled in everything from the actual work to signing autographs and doing interviews. I think that's something I learned from him. It wasn't something he said. It was the way he went about living his life in show business.

99

Jeff Bridges
More from Jeff Bridges, as he remembers the influence his father Lloyd – who passed away in 1998 – had on his acting career, *Hollywood Reporter*, June 2014

"

I told him one thing a long time ago – he's his own man, he has his own ideas – but I told him one great thing. Don't be a leading man, ever. Be a character actor and you'll work forever.

"

James Brolin
Career advice to son Josh, People.com, November 2019

66

I'm lucky for that and as you said, he's one of the greatest human beings of all time, forget actors, which he was one of the best at that too… If you knew him, you knew that you'd never meet anyone like him ever again. Special dude, man.

99

Scott Caan
Actor Scott Caan on father and Hollywood icon James Caan, People.com, January 2023

"

I adore him. I've always, always adored him. His recovery and his life is a miracle and he's an extraordinary man. We went through as you, as everyone knows I suppose, some very difficult times when he was out there. He's come back – thank heaven – and he's healthy.

"

Martin Sheen
The actor talks about son Charlie Sheen and his successful battle with drugs and alcohol, People.com, June 2021

66

He's the best training partner even though I'm starting to lift a little… I'm starting to catch up with the weights. He pushes me so much in the gym and we love training together.

99

Joseph Baena
on his perfect gym buddy – his father,
Hollywood legend Arnold Schwarzenegger!
Mirror.co.uk, June 2023

> 66
>
> The only way I can describe [fatherhood] – it sounds stupid, but – at the end of *How the Grinch Stole Christmas*, you know how his heart grows like five times? Everything is full; it's just full all the time.
>
> 99

Matt Damon
The actor connects with his inner Grinch!

"

Dad – I love you so much and I am so proud to be your son.

"

Michael Douglas
The actor's touching words after the death of
his father, Kirk Douglas. The pair having healed a
deep rift between them that had lasted many years,
Daily Express, December 2021

66

You can tell what
was the best year of your
father's life because
they seem to freeze
that clothing style and
ride it out.

99

Jerry Seinfeld

66

When I was a kid, I said to my father one afternoon, 'Daddy, will you take me to the zoo?' He answered, 'If the zoo wants you, let them come and get you.'

99

Jerry Lewis
The actor and comedian – often movie co-star of Dean Martin – with a typically amusing observation used in some of his stand-up routines

66

My son Colin, he was only like three maybe, three or four, and at the end of *The Love Boat*, it's sailing away, and they show the closing credits, and he started crying. And I said, 'Why are you crying?' He says, 'Cause you're going away on the Love Boat.' He thought I was on that boat, sailing away. It was really very sweet.

99

Tom Hanks
recalling a tender moment with son Colin,
TheThings.com, December 2022

66

I guess they were bohemians.
My father's stepfather was very
wealthy, and his money lives on,
thank you. You got money – you
can move around.

99

Keanu Reeves
on his stepfather and his family's globetrotting during
his younger years, the *Philadelphia Inquirer's* 'Keanu
Reeves: Actor Dude' by Cindy Pearlman, July 1991

"

I was a little scared by the whole thing, really. It's strange to play your own father, you know? I couldn't really wrap my mind around it.

"

Brandon Lee
explains why he opted not to take the offer of playing his late father Bruce in the 1993 biopic *Dragon: The Bruce Lee Story*, *Hollywood Reporter*, February 2018

"

Well, the first thing I think of is my dad coming to see me in a play at camp. I went to this camp in Maine, called Hidden Valley. And I hated it at first, and he came up there because I got homesick. He's a very sensitive guy, a very loving dad. My mom would be kind of like, 'No, Jerry, he's got to figure out how to be on his own.' And my dad was, like, 'No, I want to go up there and be with him.'

"

Ben Stiller
sharing a fond memory of his father Jerry Stiller,
New Yorker, May 2020

"

I grew up, somewhat, on a golf course with my dad. When I wasn't at school I was there.

"

Jason Connery
reveals what life with his father, *James Bond* star Sean, was like when he was a boy, *The Scotsman*, January 2014

66

My father was my teacher. But most importantly he was a great dad.

99

Beau Bridges
The actor pays a simple tribute to his father,
Hollywood star Lloyd Bridges, Today.com, April 2023

66

No, I am your father.

99

Darth Vadar delivers Luke Skywalker the
shocking news that he, the Dark Lord, is his
real father in *Star Wars: Episode V:
The Empire Strikes Back*, 1980

66

No, I am your father.

99

The Emperor Zurg reveals he is Buzz Lightyear's father in a hilarious parody of *Star Wars* in the Pixar classic *Toy Story 2*, Pixar.Fandom.com, 1999

66

I decided in my life that I would do nothing that did not reflect positively on my father's life.

99

Sidney Poitier
The Oscar-winning actor with the ultimate
accolade to his father

"

My father believed in toughness, honesty, politeness, and being on time. All very important lessons.

"

Roger Moore

The *James Bond* star – and quintessential English gentleman – followed his father's simple disciplines throughout his life with great dignity

I love the comic opportunities that come up in the context of a father–son relationship.

Harrison Ford
On playing both roles – son (*Indiana Jones and the Last Crusade*) and father (*Indiana Jones and the Kingdom of the Crystal Skull*)

> **66**
>
> # Do I want to be a hero to my son? No. I would like to be a very real human being. That's hard enough.
>
> **99**

Robert Downey Jr.
Ironman strives for normality over superpowers
when it comes to parenting

66

Of all my father's teachings,
the most enduring was the one
about the true measure of a man.
That true measure was how well
he provided for his children,
and it stuck with me as if it
were etched in my brain.

99

Sidney Poitier

> **"**
>
> I learned a lot in those first years in Miami, while struggling just for survival, by observing my father's fortitude.
>
> **"**

Desi Arnaz
The *I Love Lucy* co-star recalls his
father's dignity in trying times

66

With sons and fathers, there's an inexplicable connection and imprint that your father leaves on you.

99

Brad Pitt

66

The bad thing about Jack is that he is the nicest young man I have ever met in my entire life. He is too nice.

99

Michael Whitehall
Co-star of comedian Jack Whitehall's TV series *Travels With My Father* suggests his son needs a harder edge to take his career to the next level, Mirror.co.uk, January 2023

CHAPTER FOUR

WALK THIS WAY

Singers and musicians wax lyrical
about the special relationship
between dads and their lads…

66

We have basically decided, without any great decision, to be with our baby (Shaun) as much as we can until we feel we can take time off to indulge ourselves in creating things outside of the family.

99

John Lennon
In 1977, the former Beatle revealed his plan to take a hiatus from music and raise his baby son Shaun, SmoothRadio.com, June 2022

❝

After my dad died, one of
the ways in which I mourned
or processed his death was just
listening to that record over
and over again.

❞

Shaun Lennon
Talking about his coping methods after his dad John
had been assassinated in New York – mainly listening
to the song he had written about Shaun, "Beautiful
Boy", SmoothRadio.com, June 2022

The seven "disciplines" of raising a son...

As a father, you must be a provider, protector, leader, teacher, helper, encourager, and friend.

> ❝
> I've never said goodbye
> to my dad, because
> I couldn't let go of him.
> ❞

Matt Monro Jr.
The son of international singing star, Matt Monro, talks
about dealing with his father's untimely passing aged
54, DailyRecord.co.uk, October 2018

66
Money can't buy life.
99

Bob Marley
The reggae star's poignant final message to son
Ziggy before he passed away in May 1981,
Far Out Magazine, October 2022

66

I think for me what I learned from my father most being around him, is a way of having principles and living up to those principles and standing up for your principles. His example is a good example for me… selflessness, charity, and standing up for what you believe and having principles. Spirituality, too.

99

Ziggy Marley
reflecting on his late father's influences,
Grammy.com, June 2018

66

If a son is uneducated, his father is to blame.

99

Chinese proverb

66

By the time a man realizes that maybe his father was right, he usually has a son who thinks he's wrong.

99

Charles Wadsworth
The classical pianist, no doubt speaking
from experience!

"

Fatherhood is super scary.
Because you don't know what the
hell you're doing. But you figure
things out as you go. It does give
your life a different meaning,
and lights you up in a way that
you never imagined.

"

Justin Timberlake

66

I just sit there and make up songs and sing to [my son] in gibberish. I'm very good at gibberish now.

99

Elton John
The Rocket Man opens a new chapter in songwriting

66

My father was a man of
love. He always loved me to
death… I don't even remember a
really cross, unkind word
from my father.

99

Johnny Cash
Legendary singer reveals he never had to
walk the line with his father

66

With Enrique, it's not a question of singing, it's a question of aptitude. He has the blood, the spirit, the character of a champion. you go into a fight with Enrique boxing, he'd kill you.

99

Julio Iglesias
The legendary singer talks about son Enrique – and advises against boxing him! HuffingtonPost.com, November 2012

"

You got right to the head of why people have a problem with me. If people want to talk about Bob Dylan, I can talk about that. But my dad belongs to me and four other people exclusively. I'm very protective of that. And telling people whether he was affectionate is telling people a lot. It has so little to do with me. I come up against a wall.

"

Jakob Dylan
Talking about his father Bob Dylan – and why he (rightly) rarely mentions what he deems as private information, *New York Times*, May 2005

66

Our relationship was getting better
before he died. He was in a happier
place. He wanted to reconnect, not just
with me but with the rest of his family.
He never got a chance to do so. Even
now, almost 40 years after he died,
I hold my father's memory dear.

99

Julian Lennon
Recalling how his relationship with estranged father
John was mending around the time of his murder in
New York, CosmicMagazine.com

66

If I have a problem, stuff's
going through my head, I feel
like using, I usually go and talk
to my dad… I decided to get
sober a lot younger than he did.
He first tried to get sober when
he was like 32, I believe.

99

Jack Osbourne
talking about his candid relationship
with dad Ozzy, *AZ Quotes*

66

My son Jack once said to me,
'Dad, do you think people are
laughing with you or at you?'
And I said, 'I don't care as
long as they're laughing.'

99

Ozzy Osbourne
The Times, December 2003

❝

I wasn't anything special as a father. But I loved them, and they knew it.

❞

Sammy Davies Jr.
The Rat Pack star and entertainer extraordinaire admits he may have had his shortcomings as a parent, but loving his three sons wasn't one of them.

66

The fact that my
relationship with my
son is so good makes me
forgiving of my father
and also appreciative.

99

Anthony Kiedis
The Red Hot Chili Peppers lead singer in a
retrospective mood over his past and present

CHAPTER FIVE

SAME GOALS

Sporting legends:
Dads
and their Lads

66

It's one of the best days of my life. First of all, congratulations on Bronny and the decision he made…super proud of him…our family is proud of him. For me, personally, it's even more special to me 'cause it's the first time someone out of my family to go to college. Obviously I didn't go to college either so it's just a proud moment to see my son go to college and he's the first one to go to college in my family so super, duper proud. Super emotional.

99

LeBron James
LA Lakers basketball star on his son Bronny's decision to go to college, *Daily Mail*, May 2023

66

I am most proud of my family, especially my father. He taught me the game, and he taught me how to play it the right way.

99

Ken Griffey Jr.
The baseball Hall of Fame inductee
on his favourite teacher

As of May 2023, it was estimated that there are 1.5 billion fathers in the world.

That's a lot of potential Father's Day cards...

66

I went night fishing with my dad instead. I just felt too young to party. I was 17. So I thought it was the most sensible thing to do and Vinny (Kompany) actually said it was the right call. Funnily enough, we didn't talk much about the football, we just chatted about normal dad and son stuff. He is a United fan. He is finding it difficult this year...

99

Phil Foden
Manchester City and England forward explains why he didn't celebrate with his City team-mates after winning the Premier League in 2019, BeSoccer.com, May 2019

66

My dad was my hero.
He showed me the
way to play this game
with respect, integrity,
and class.

99

Barry Bonds
San Francisco Giants baseball legend
on the bonds that tie

66

When I was a little boy,
I didn't know what the
Hall of Fame was. I was
just playing the game of
baseball, and I wanted to
be just like my dad.

99

Roberto Alomar
Toronto Blue Jays legend cites his main
influence on his career

66

I grew up in a small town in Illinois, and my dad was a basketball coach. Thanks to him, I have excellent fundamentals in both basketball and baseball.

99

Nick Offerman
US actor and comedian reveals his dad's talents could have led him down a more sporting path

66

There's something special in baseball that connects generations, from father to son.

99

Pedro Martínez
Former Boston Red Sox pitcher on the unbreakable
bonds between father and son that baseball
seems to nurture so well

66

Dad taught me everything I know. Unfortunately, he didn't teach me everything he knows.

99

Al Unser Jr.
The US racing driver, part of the Unser driving dynasty, who did well with limited knowledge!

66

If the father is a tiger, then the son will also be a tiger.

99

Chinese proverb

66

There's a big commitment that your parents make, and my dad made every commitment to me. There was never a moment where he didn't have time to support what I wanted to do.

99

Tom Brady

66

My father used to say that it's never too late to do anything you wanted to do. And he said, 'You never know what you can accomplish until you try.'

99

Michael Jordan

66

If my son is happy, then I am happy.

99

Chris Paul
Veteran NBA star "CP3" outlines his personal
happiness blueprint

66

My father taught me
a good lesson: Don't get too low
when things go wrong.
And don't get too high when
things are good.

99

Robert Parish
NBA legend and Boston Celts star recalls his
father's poignant words

"

I am very proud. It's great to see. He has always loved the Premier League and it's been a dream of his for a long time. I enjoy when he smiles and when he celebrates the goals of his team-mates, it's great to see.

"

Alf-Inge Haaland
Norwegian ex-footballer reflects on a magical first season for his son Erling Haaland at Manchester City, mancity.com, May 2023

> ## 66
>
> We've always talked a lot
> about football ever since
> I started playing. We still do.
> For my whole life, he has
> been a big role model.
>
> ## 99

Erling Haaland
on his father Alf-Inge Haaland's influence,
FourFourTwo.com

66

My dad is an obvious help and a massive influence on my game. Sometimes it is a case of 'enough about rugby' and we do speak about lots of other things. I learn a lot from so many different people – on and off the pitch – and my dad is a huge part of that process.

99

Owen Farrell
The England rugby union star on father Andy, head coach of the Ireland rugby union team, *Evening Standard*, May 2011

66

My dad's actions were probably what kind of moulded me not only in a footballing sense, but in a life way as well.

99

Frank Lampard
The former England and Chelsea football star talks
about the tough love his father, Frank Lampard Senior,
gave him as a kid, *The Sun*, September 2020

> **"**
>
> They saw Kasper for what he is and saw his qualities not just as a footballer but also as a human being, and the leadership qualities that he's always possessed and the value that he could give to not only the dressing room but the whole football club. I'm very, very proud of what he has done because it's difficult.
>
> **"**

Peter Schmeichel
The former Manchester United goalkeeper talks about son Kapser and how his move to Leicester City helped him develop into a top goalkeeper for club and country, LeicesterMercury.co.uk, April 2023

66

To a son, his dad is the greatest dad on earth. To a father, his kid is the greatest kid on earth.

99

Unknown

"

If I play well and if I have a
chance to win, that's great. But
it's not at the forefront of my
mind, put it that way. I'm here
to have a good week with my
dad and enjoy it.

"

Rory McIlroy
Ahead of a tournament, golfer Rofy McIlroy
puts fun with dad Gerry over silverware,
The Scotsman, September 2022

66

I've got a picture of him hitting a ball when he is one year, nine months old and wearing cords and a sweater knitted by his mother! I caddied for Rory and travelled all over Ireland and the States with him, but I learned to give him space. I've seen parents ruin good golfers.

99

Gerry McIlroy
on giving his golfer son Rory space as and when needed, *Daily Mail*, 2009

66

My father gave me the greatest gift anyone could give another person: He believed in me.

99

Jim Valvano
The former basketball star on his father's influence
on him, Today.com, April 2023

66

Anyone can be a father, but it takes someone special to be a dad, and that's why I call you dad, because you are so special to me. You taught me the game and you taught me how to play it right.

99

Wade Boggs
Boston Red Sox legend reveals where his stellar career first began... with his dad, Parentacoms blog

66

Becoming a dad means you have to be a role model for your son and be someone he can look up to.

99

Wayne Rooney
The former England and Manchester United star,
taking fatherhood as seriously as he did his
football career, Supanet.com

66

Of all the titles I've been privileged to have, 'Dad' has always been the best.

99

Ken Norton
Former World champion boxer – and dad

CHAPTER SIX

SAME SCRIPT

More words
of wisdom from all
walks of life…

"

A son is the clearest reflection of his father in the world.

"

Unknown

66

Father's love will always be imprinted on the heart of a son.

99

Unknown

The concept of Father's Day was invented by Sonora Smart Dodd, who was from Washington, USA. Her father single-handedly raised his six children after their mother died in childbirth.

June was her dad's birthday month so it made sense to start Father's Day then – it would soon catch on and eventually become a worldwide day of celebration.

66

Even in the best father-son relationships, there's an uncomfortable familiarity that inhibits us from talking like friends.

99

Joe Kita
The *Men's Health* writer may be on to something!

66

I went to public schools in Bangor, Maine and had as normal a childhood as you could imagine someone could, living in an enormous red house and being the son of a millionaire best-selling writer. I mean I actually had a strangely normal childhood despite all that.

99

Owen King
The author on his relatively normal upbringing with his father, the best-selling author Stephen King, *Entertainment Weekly*, September 2017

"

I killed the monsters.
That's what fathers do.

"

F. K. Wallace

> **"**
>
> # Fathering is not something perfect men do, but something that perfects the man.
>
> **"**

Frank Pittman
Psychiatrist, author and columnist, the late Frank Pittman of "Ask Dr Frank" fame sums up fatherhood in one simple sentence, Today.com, April 2023

66

How come my three-year-old son knows every species and genus of dinosaur and I can't even remember my home phone number?

99

Taye Diggs
The US actor highlights his son's monstrous ability to retain information compared with his own memory issues

Ten modern father and son songs

1. "Hey Dad" by Tyler Booth (Country – 2022)
2. "Old Man" by Beck (Rock – 2022)
3. "What Makes a Man" by Ben Rector & Thomas Rhett (Pop – 2022)
4. "Good Ol' Man" by Drew Green (Country – 2022)
5. "You Will Always Be My Son" by Caleb and Kelsey (Pop – 2022)
6. "Like You" by Aaron Cole, Tauren Wells, and TobyMac (Christian – 2021)
7. "My Son" by Eddie Montgomery (Country – 2021)
8. "Stay at Home Dad" by Drew Baldridge (Country – 2021)
9. "Dad" by Coleton Rubin (Rock – 2021)
10. "Things Dads Do" by Thomas Rhett (Country – 2021)

"

Barney Walsh: 'The memories you make doing these things, and being with you, we are so blessed to be able to do this thing.'

Bradley Walsh: 'Yeah, you're right, I just think it's, very, umm… It's just a lovely thing to do, it's just amazing.'

"

A touching moment as Barney Walsh and his father, long-time presenter of 'The Chase', Bradley Walsh, discuss the making of their latest 'Breaking Dad' adventure for UK channel ITV, *Daily Express*, June 2023

66

Literally, the reason I chose *Gogglebox* is that I know that when I'm older and when he's not here anymore, I can say to my kids and my grandkids 'this was the relationship I had with my dad.' So that's why I do it.

99

Roman Kemp
The BBC Radio 1 DJ explains the real reason behind his decision to appear on Channel 4 show *Gogglebox* – to be with his dad Martin, Tyla.com, July 2022

"

Nothing is dearer to an ageing father than his son.

"

Unknown

> **"**
>
> My father raised us
> to step toward trouble
> rather than to step
> away from it.
>
> **"**

Justin Trudeau

66

Don't wait until your son is a man to make him great; make him great as a boy.

99

Unknown

66

A father is a man who expects his son to be as good a man as he meant to be.

99

Frank A. Clark

66

Forget Batman: When
I really thought about
what I wanted to be
when I grew up, I
wanted to be my dad.

99

Paul Asay
The journalist, author, and movie critic on his
super-powered father

66

A father is neither an anchor to hold us back nor a sail to take us there but a guiding light whose love shows us the way.

99

Unknown

66

We became friends, not just father and son.

99

Richard Bergeron
Canadian politician on his
special relationship with his son

> 66
>
> The older a man gets,
> the more he values
> everything his dad
> gave him.
>
> 99
>
> **Unknown**

66

My dad is my best friend, my father, and my boss. When I do something that is exciting and he likes it, it feels three times as good, as you can imagine.

99

David Lauren
US businessman and youngest son of
Ralph Lauren on his role-model father

No matter
how tall a son
grows, he will
always look up
to his dad.

Unknown

"

How can we expect our
boys to become powerful,
successful, and complete men
if we ourselves don't possess or
act on the tools and the know-
how to take them there?

"

Eric Davis
The former Cincinnati Reds baseball star
asks a poignant question

> **"**
>
> My father didn't tell me how to live; he lived, and let me watch him do it.
>
> **"**

Clarence B. Kelland
The prolific American writer on the importance of fathers teaching by example

66

Listen, there is no way any true man is
going to let children live around him
in his home and not discipline and
teach, fight, and mould them until they
know all he knows. His goal is to make
them better than he is. Being their
friend is a distant second to this.

99

Victor Devlin

66

It takes great courage to love unconditionally.

99

Isaac Mogilevsky
The filmmaker, author, and speaker, writer of
*A Letter to My Father: What Your Son Wants to
Tell You But Doesn't*

66

Tell me who your
father is, and I'll tell
you who you are.

99

Filipino proverb

66

Each parent talks about the waking up during the night and the feeding during the night, but for me that was the most special time. It doesn't matter what time of the night it is or how tired you are, they make you smile, they make you happy.

99

David Beckham
Inter Miami stakeholder and former England star on the magical night hours

66

A good father is one of the most
unsung, unpraised, unnoticed,
and yet one of the most valuable
assets in our society.

99

Billy Graham
The American evangelist – never a truer word spoken

66

When the father has eaten too much salt in his lifetime, then his son thereafter will have a great thirst.

99

Vietnamese proverb

66

What is the son but an extension of the father?

99

Frank Herbert
US author of sci-fi classic *Dune*

> ❝
>
> We think our fathers
> fools, so wise we grow.
> Our wiser sons, no
> doubt will think us so.
>
> ❞

Alexander Pope
The English poet shares his thoughts on the
father-and-son relationship

66

To my son, never forget that I
love you. Life is filled with hard
times and good times. Learn
from everything you can. Be the
man I know you can be.

99

Unknown

66

A son is not a judge
of his father, but the
conscience of the father
is in his son.

99

Simon Soloveychik
So says the Russian philosopher

66

The guiding light of
my father has proven
to be the brightest star
in the sky.

99

Unknown

66

Father and son relationships
can be complicated – mine
certainly is. Love. Hate. Respect.
Fear. Worship. Disdain. Pride.
Disappointment. Happiness.
Anger. Joy. Sadness.

The list goes on.

99

John H. Clark III
The award-winning journalist tries to figure out the
complexity of father-and-son relationships

"

One father can feed
seven children, but
seven children cannot
feed one father.

"

Cameroonian proverb

66

Lately all of my friends are worried that they're turning into their fathers. I'm worried that I'm not.

99

Dan Zevin
US humourist and author swims against the fatherly tide

66

Like father, like son: every good tree makes good fruits.

99

William Langland
English poet William Langland makes a
simple but often salient observation

"

Like father, like son.

"

Latin proverb